Original title:
Translucent Sparks Over the Fae Graft

Copyright © 2025 Swan Charm
All rights reserved.

Author: Mirell Mesipuu
ISBN HARDBACK: 978-1-80562-010-5
ISBN PAPERBACK: 978-1-80563-531-4

The Sparkling Veil in Electric Hues

In twilight's dance, the shadows play,
With whispers soft, they drift away.
A curtain hung of colors bright,
Where dreams emerge in fading light.

The stars awake with gentle grace,
Illuminating time and space.
Each twinkle sings a tale forlorn,
Of magic born and love reborn.

The forest hums with ancient lore,
As magic stirs upon the shore.
Beneath the veil, the worlds unite,
In sparkling hues, a dazzling sight.

The moonbeams race through silver trees,
Caressing leaves with tender ease.
A moment's peace, a heart's delight,
In whispers shared beneath the night.

So linger here, a while, my friend,
Where time and dreams seem never end.
In every hue, a promise glows,
The magic of the world bestows.

Dancing Fancies in Celestial Fields

In fields where starlight weaves a thread,
The dreams awake, their colors spread.
With whispers soft, the winds do play,
In cosmic dance, the night turns day.

Each flower blooms with laughter bright,
As shadows twirl in silver light.
Beneath the moon's soft, watchful gaze,
Creation sings in wondrous ways.

The paths of fortune twist and gleam,
Like ribbons spun from hope's own dream.
With every step, the heart takes flight,
In celestial realms, all feels right.

A waltz of magic fills the air,
A tapestry beyond compare.
With every twirl, a world we find,
In dancing fancies, joy unconfined.

So join the revelry tonight,
In fields where dreams take boundless flight.
In every heart, a spark ignites,
In stellar realms, we soar to heights.

Moonlit Fragments of Magic's Embrace

Under the veil of silken skies,
Where clouds like whispers softly rise,
The moon casts light on ancient ground,
In fragments lost, our dreams are found.

Each shimmering ray a tale untold,
In silver hues, our hopes unfold.
The night unfolds with secrets sweet,
In magic's arms, our souls do meet.

With every glance, a spark ignites,
Beneath the stars, we chase the nights.
In shadows deep, enchantments weave,
In dreams we dare, we learn to believe.

The world drifts by in shimmered hues,
Each sigh and laughter, a gentle muse.
In moonlit realms where time stands still,
Magic dances, bending will.

Embrace the fragments, let them flow,
In every moment, let love grow.
In twilight's arms, together stay,
In moonlit realms, we find our way.

Glistening Miracles in Mystic Hours

In whispered tones, the night unfolds,
With glistening dreams and tales retold.
Each hour a miracle, softly spun,
Under the gaze of the midnight sun.

The stars align in rhythmic grace,
In mystic hours, we trace their face.
With every heartbeat, magic thrives,
In wonder's glow, enchantment drives.

The forest breathes in twilight's hue,
With secrets shared among the few.
In shadows deep, we seek the light,
A journey born from sheer delight.

With every moment, time suspends,
As magic whispers, and the heart mends.
In glistening dreams, we find our way,
Through mystic hours, night turns to day.

So let us wander, hand in hand,
Through fields of stars, a dreamland grand.
In glistening miracles, we find our song,
In mystic hours, where we belong.

Enchanted Reflections in Crystal Waters

In crystal waters, dreams take flight,
Reflections shimmer in soft moonlight.
The world below, a mystery vast,
In quiet depths, our shadows cast.

With every ripple, stories blend,
In enchanted whispers, paths extend.
The gentle sway of water's kiss,
Brings forth a magic, pure bliss.

Each pond a portal to realms unknown,
In tranquil moments, love has grown.
The surface glints like stars aflame,
In crystal waters, we find our name.

As night descends, a tapestry bright,
With every glance, we chase the night.
In stillness deep, our hearts connect,
In enchanted reflections, we introspect.

So let us dive, let spirits soar,
In crystal waters, forevermore.
In every wave, a tale awaits,
In enchanted realms, we find our fates.

Veils of Glow in Elven Heartlands

In twilight's embrace, the shadows dance,
Whispers of magic in every glance.
Elven hearts beat soft and true,
Veils of glow in the silvery dew.

Beneath the stars, the night unfurls,
Dreams of wonder in secret swirls.
Crickets sing with ancient grace,
In this enchanted, timeless place.

A river flows with secrets deep,
Where time itself seems fast asleep.
Glowing embers flutter and weave,
Crafting beauty that none can believe.

In every leaf, a story hums,
Echoes of joy as twilight comes.
Candles of starlight softly gleam,
Guiding wishes, crafting dreams.

With laughter light as fairy dust,
Elven folk weave their bonds of trust.
In heartlands where the soft winds sigh,
Veils of glow shall never die.

Dappled Glimmers in the Enchanted Grove

In the grove where the sunlight spills,
Dappled glimmers dance and swells.
A symphony of leaves so bright,
Whispers echo in pure delight.

Squirrels twirl in playful chase,
Nimble feet in a fragrant space.
Mushrooms blink in a secret show,
Carpets of magic in the flow.

Petals drift on a gentle breeze,
Nature's laughter among the trees.
Sunbeams kiss the emerald floor,
In this grove, we seek for more.

Mystic creatures softly tread,
Guided by the stars ahead.
In moonlit beams, their secrets hide,
Dappled glimmers, their cherished pride.

As twilight wraps its soft embrace,
We find our way through this wild space.
With hearts aglow like fireflies,
In the enchanted grove, our spirits rise.

Spectral Flashes Beneath the Ancient Boughs

Beneath the boughs where shadows play,
Spectral flashes light the way.
Whispers of history in the air,
Ancient echoes weave everywhere.

The forest breathes with soft replies,
Mysteries twinkle in ageless sighs.
Each rustle hints of stories untold,
In sacred woods, the brave and bold.

A flicker here, a shimmer there,
Ghostly forms move without a care.
Gnarled branches stretch towards the night,
Guardians of dreams, hidden from sight.

In the stillness, secrets unfold,
The magic of night, both tender and bold.
With every flicker, our spirits rise,
Spectral flashes beneath dark skies.

And when dawn breaks, the shadows fade,
The whispers of night forever stay made.
For in these woods, all hearts are free,
Among spectres of memory, we find our glee.

Flickering Whimsy in the Realm of Mist

In realms where the morning mist does cling,
Flickering whimsy makes the heart sing.
Soft echoes weave through the chilled air,
Painting dreams with delicate care.

Faeries dance in the pale moonlight,
Veils of fog twisting, a wondrous sight.
Their laughter rings like chimes of gold,
Stories of wonders yet to be told.

Wandering paths of twisting light,
Lead us to realms of pure delight.
A sprinkle of magic, a hint of grace,
In the misty realm, we find our place.

As shadows twirl, the world transforms,
Flickering whimsy in countless forms.
Each step we take, new tales arise,
In this mystical realm, where enchantment lies.

Embrace the unseen, let spirits guide,
In mists of wonder, forever abide.
For every flicker is a chance to roam,
In the realm of mist, we find our home.

The Flicker of Magic in Whispering Woods

In the woods where shadows play,
Whispers weave through branches sway.
A flicker bright, a spark anew,
Magic swirls in emerald hue.

Moonlit paths, where secrets dwell,
Echoes of an ancient spell.
Elusive sprites in twilight sing,
Through the air, their laughter ring.

Leaves of gold in gentle breeze,
Dancing softly, nature's ease.
Amidst the trees, a world so grand,
Where dreams are born and hopes withstand.

Time suspends its hurried flow,
As fantasy begins to grow.
Every heart finds peace and rest,
In the woods, forever blessed.

So linger here, let worries fade,
In this realm, adventure made.
The flicker glows, a timeless guide,
In whispering woods, let magic bide.

Glistening Wonders in Twilight's Embrace

In twilight's grasp, the world transforms,
Glistening wonders, beauty warms.
Stars awaken, shy but bright,
Painting dreams in the softening light.

Rivers of silver, flowing slow,
Nature's palette begins to glow.
Each heartbeat echoes in the night,
As shadows dance in soft moonlight.

Gentle breezes carry tales,
Of ancient lands and distant sails.
Creatures stir, both small and grand,
In the twilight, hand in hand.

Petals shimmer with dew's embrace,
Every blossom finds its place.
In whispers shared between the trees,
Magic lingers in the evening breeze.

So join the dance, let whispers soar,
In twilight's arms, forevermore.
The wonders gleam, the night ignites,
In this embrace, our souls take flight.

Shining Facets of the Faerie Dance

Underneath the silver moon,
Faeries gather, hearts in tune.
Shining facets, twinkling light,
Graceful forms in joyous flight.

Wings of gossamer, bright and fair,
Spinning tales on the midnight air.
They weave a spell, enchanting, bright,
The magic glows, a wondrous sight.

Whirls of laughter, sparks in the night,
Every movement pure delight.
In a circle, round they go,
To the rhythm of nature's flow.

Softly ringing, chimes of cheer,
The faerie dance draws all so near.
A tapestry of dreams unfurled,
In this moment, a sacred world.

So take a step, let worries cease,
Join the dance, embrace the peace.
In shining facets, magic sways,
In faerie dances, endless days.

Ethereal Echoes Beyond the Grove

Beyond the grove, where silence breathes,
Ethereal echoes weave through leaves.
Mysteries linger on the air,
A tapestry of dreams laid bare.

Footsteps soft on ancient ground,
Whispers of secrets, long profound.
In shadows deep, the memories grow,
Of stories told, of things we know.

Crickets sing a lilting song,
Nature's chorus, pure and strong.
Every note a gentle call,
Inviting souls to heed its thrall.

Time drifts softly, moments blend,
In the grove, where pathways mend.
Memories glow like distant stars,
Guiding hearts through night's memoirs.

So linger here, let echoes guide,
Through the grove, where dreams abide.
In ethereal whispers, we find light,
Beyond the grove, into the night.

Chasing Glowworms through the Fey Forest

In the depths where the wild things play,
Tiny lights flicker, leading the way.
Whispers of secrets in the midnight air,
Beneath the canopy, magic lays bare.

Branches sway softly, a curious tune,
Glowworms twinkle like stars in the gloom.
A chase through the shadows, a dance in the night,
Each flicker a promise, pure delight.

Sprightly laughter echoes, joyous and free,
Following trails of soft luminescent glee.
In the heart of the forest, where dreams intertwine,
Nature's own lanterns, a sight so divine.

Moss carpets the ground, a cushion of green,
In this ethereal realm, I've never seen.
Lost in the wonder, with each little spark,
The Fey Forest glows like a luminous ark.

As dawn beckons softly, the glow begins to fade,
Yet the magic remains, in the memories made.
Bound by the moment, with spirits uplifted,
In chasing the glowworms, my heart is gifted.

Elixirs of Radiance in Luminous Realms

In a cauldron bubbling under silver moons,
Elixirs of radiance, sweet earthy tunes.
Bottles aglow, shimmering bright,
Promises hidden in the soft, golden light.

Spilled on the ground, they weave and they twine,
Crafting a tapestry, divine and benign.
Each swirl a potion, each sip a flight,
To worlds of enchantment, hidden from sight.

With whispers of fairies that flutter and sing,
The essence of magic begins to take wing.
In luminous realms where the shadows retreat,
Each elixir sparkles, a liquid heartbeat.

Through a garden of crystals, so vivid and rare,
Wonders await us, if only we dare.
In the heart of the night, as the stars convene,
We sip on the laughter of realms yet unseen.

Awash in the glow of our fantastical fate,
We drink in the magic, our hearts palpitate.
With each drop of starlight, together we soar,
In this luminous journey, forever we explore.

Sylphs of Light Dancing with Shadows

Underneath the boughs where the moonlight plays,
Sylphs weave their dance through the night's soft haze.
With gossamer wings, they flutter and glide,
In a realm where the shadows and starlight collide.

Whirls of bright laughter fill the cool night air,
As patterns of light weave a tapestry rare.
Their movements are whispers, a delicate grace,
In a ballroom of nature, they twirl and embrace.

Each sylph a spark, each shadow a friend,
A cosmic connection that knows no end.
As they leap through the darkness, a luminous thread,
The dance of the sylphs beckons dreams to spread.

In corners of twilight where secrets reside,
Their laughter ignites and the shadows slide.
Together they dance on the edge of the night,
Creating a symphony, pure and alight.

So join in the revel, let your spirit take flight,
With sylphs of light dancing, banishing fright.
Lose yourself in the rhythm, in wonder, behold,
The beauty of magic in stories retold.

Glimmers of Enchantment in Hidden Thickets

In thickets concealed, where the brambles entwine,
Glimmers of enchantment in shadows they shine.
A rustle of leaves, a flicker of gold,
Whispers of legends and tales to be told.

Amongst tangled roots where the wildflowers bloom,
The air thick with magic, sweet fragrance, a plume.
Each shimmer a story of love and of lore,
In hidden thickets, there's always more.

Through the overgrown paths where the moonbeams peek,

A maze of delight that the heart dares to seek.
In the silence of night, with the stars brushing near,
Glimmers of enchantment bring hope ever clear.

The echoes of laughter, a delicate tease,
With each breath from the forest, freedom to seize.
Nature's own tapestry, rich and profound,
In the thickets where mysteries are joyously found.

So wander, dear friend, into twilight's embrace,
Let the glimmers lead you, with whimsical grace.
With each step you take, let your spirit be free,
In hidden thickets, find the magic in we.

Luminescent Trails of Forgotten Paths

In the hush of night, secrets call,
Where moonbeams whisper, shadows fall.
Stars are sprinkled on the ground,
Lost roads paved with magic found.

Echoes of laughter, long since stored,
Through tangled bramble, fate restored.
Each step taken, a story weaves,
Among the dreams the starlight leaves.

Memories flicker, dimly bright,
Guiding the wanderer's weary sight.
A gentle breath of time's embrace,
Illuminates the hidden place.

With every path that time has worn,
Old sorrows fade, new hopes are born.
In luminescent trails we trust,
To lead us through, as stardust must.

The journey calls, let courage rise,
Embrace the night and the endless skies.
For in these trails, both wild and free,
Lies the heart of our history.

Veil of Light Among the Faeries

Beneath the boughs where moonlight sways,
The faeries weave their silvery plays.
With laughter soft as summer rain,
They greet the dusk, not one in vain.

A veil of light, a shimmered glow,
Dances on petals, 'neath the bow.
Secrets of magic, whispered low,
In every breeze, the stories flow.

In twilight's arms, they flit and glide,
With wings aglow, they gently bide.
A world unseen, just out of reach,
They teach the heart what words can't teach.

With eyes like stars, they spark the night,
Bringing forth dreams, pure and bright.
A fleeting glimpse, then away they fly,
Leaving hopes to shimmer and sigh.

So listen close, when shadows gleam,
For faeries dwell in every dream.
Among the light, their laughter calls,
Awake, dear heart, when evening falls.

Aetherial Glimmers in the Heart of the Forest

In the heart where shadows blend,
A light like laughter, soft descend.
Glimmers twinkle, a spark divine,
Telling secrets through the pine.

Murmurs of magic, wild and free,
Dance on the wind, a gentle spree.
Leaves shimmer green, underfoot,
In every cranny, wonder's root.

Ancient trees with stories rife,
Hold the pulse of woodland life.
Aetherial whispers in the air,
Point the way to treasures rare.

Through bramble thick and paths untrod,
Nature sings of love, though flawed.
Each footfall sings a silent sound,
In the enchanted woods, we're bound.

With every breath the forest breathes,
Comes the promise that it weaves.
In emerald halls, our spirits roam,
For here, dear friend, we find our home.

The Dance of Light and Shadow

In twilight's embrace, the shadows sway,
Dancing with light at the end of day.
A gentle waltz, two souls in flight,
Across the canvas of fading light.

Whispers echo in the dusk's soft kiss,
Each moment savored, a fleeting bliss.
Light twirls brightly, shadow retreats,
In every heartbeat, the magic repeats.

Stars awaken, flickering bright,
Guiding the dance into the night.
In every flicker, the stories blend,
Where light and shadow lovingly mend.

Each step taken, a tale to tell,
In the dance of dusk, all hearts swell.
For in this moment, we feel alive,
Both darkness and light, together thrive.

So hold onto dreams as the night draws near,
In the dance of life, there's nothing to fear.
Light and shadow, a perfect pair,
In every step, find love and care.

Luminous Visions Beneath the Ancient Oak

In shadows deep, where whispers play,
An ancient oak holds secrets sway.
Its roots entwined with stories old,
In every knot, a dream unfolds.

Beneath its boughs, the starlight spills,
A symphony of night-time thrills.
The fireflies dance, a fleeting show,
In this enchanted, timeless glow.

The winds weave tales of long ago,
Of magic realms where wonders flow.
Each rustling leaf a voice refined,
In nature's book, the heart entwined.

With every sigh that breezes through,
The oak remembers, ever true.
In nature's calm, where spirits meet,
The world holds secrets, bittersweet.

Beneath the stars, a wish can bloom,
In ancient glades, dispelling gloom.
So sit awhile, and close your eyes,
For visions live when silence sighs.

The Sparkle of Secrets in Twilight

As daylight fades to dusky hues,
The world unfurls its evening views.
With twilight's kiss, the air turns gold,
A tapestry of stories told.

Upon the cobblestones of fate,
The whispers linger, never wait.
A sparkle here, a glance that drifts,
In the twilight, magic lifts.

The secrets hidden in shadows creep,
Where dreams awaken from their sleep.
Each pulse of light, a spark of grace,
In this enchanted, twilight space.

Beneath the arch of fading light,
The stars prepare to crown the night.
With every twinkle, hearts align,
In twilight's grasp, our souls combine.

As night befalls, the world grows still,
Let magic guide your heart and will.
In every shadow, wonder waits,
For twilight weaves its woven fates.

Wandering Lights in Mystic Groves

In the groves where secrets hide,
Wandering lights in silence glide.
They beckon forth the hearts once lost,
Amidst the pines, no matter the cost.

With every step, the magic grows,
Beneath the moon, the soft wind blows.
Each flicker shines like dreams of old,
In mystic woods, the stories unfold.

The echoes of a time that's past,
Dance in the night, forever cast.
A chorus sung by spirits near,
In wandering lights that draw us near.

They weave a path through slumbering trees,
Where whispered secrets drift with ease.
To chase the glow, our spirits soar,
With every flicker, we seek for more.

In the heart of nature's vault,
These lights reveal our deepest thoughts.
Wandering free, our souls ignite,
In mystic groves, where hearts take flight.

Enchanted Glow of Whispering Willows

Beneath the weeping willow's grace,
An enchanted glow finds its place.
With branches swaying in soft delight,
The stars peer down to bless the night.

In rustling leaves, the stories hum,
Of timeless love, where spirits come.
Each sigh a promise, tender, true,
In twilight's arms, begin anew.

The moon spills silver on the ground,
In gentle waves, the world unbound.
With every whispered secret shared,
The willow listens, always spared.

As night unfolds, the magic glows,
In dreams unfurling, softly flows.
With every flicker, each heart knows,
The quiet wonders nature shows.

In the embrace of night's soft fold,
The willows weave their tales of old.
In whispered breezes, hope does swell,
As dreams entwine beneath their spell.

Shimmering Lore of the Woodland Spirits

In the hush of ancient trees,
Whispers float like fireflies,
Stories spun on silver breeze,
Dreams alight in verdant sighs.

Spirits dance in moonlight's gaze,
Casting spells of timeless grace,
Guided by the night's soft haze,
They weave magic in this place.

From the roots to winding boughs,
Life entwines with nature's art,
Echoes of forgotten vows,
Hum in every beating heart.

Beneath the ferns and glowing mist,
Secret paths and hidden springs,
In this realm, we can't resist,
The charm that every spirit brings.

So listen close, and you will find,
Visions dancing in your mind,
Woodland spirits, intertwined,
In shimmering lore, we're aligned.

Glowing Legends in the Faerie Flare

In dusk's embrace, the faeries rise,
With laughter that ignites the night,
Glowing legends in their eyes,
Hold the tales of pure delight.

They flit and flutter, bright and bold,
Painting dreams in vibrant hues,
Whispers of adventures old,
In every twinkle, they enthuse.

Beneath the veil of starlit skies,
They scatter joy with every flight,
In their path, the magic lies,
As shadows dance in soft moonlight.

With gossamer wings and glowing threads,
They spin the world with daring flair,
And every wave that wisdom spreads,
Creates a bond beyond compare.

So wander close to where they play,
Let the faerie magic flare,
In glowing legends, come what may,
An echo of the purest care.

Magical Threads Beneath the Starry Skies

Underneath the velvet dome,
Where twinkling stars weave dreams anew,
Magical threads, a celestial home,
Guide the wanderers in their view.

Cosmic whispers in the air,
As stardust falls on earth so bright,
Each spark a tale, a wish laid bare,
A tapestry of hope and light.

In the silence of the night,
The universe unfolds its lore,
While shadows weave in soft twilight,
Pulling heartstrings evermore.

Beneath the depth of endless skies,
We find our place amidst the glow,
As constellations softly rise,
A guiding map for us to know.

So take a breath, and look above,
At magical threads that interlace,
In every night, there shines a love,
Connecting us through time and space.

Illuminated Dreams of Sylvan Twilight

In the folds of velvety night,
Sylvan dreams begin to bloom,
With whispers soft and colors bright,
Illuminating every room.

Through dew-kissed leaves, the magic flows,
As twilight weaves its gentle spell,
Each petal wrapped in sweet repose,
A serene world where wishes dwell.

Beneath the gaze of watching stars,
The forest holds its breath in glee,
For every wish, no matter how far,
Transforms into a melody.

From the roots to the sky's embrace,
Dreams unfold in shimmering hues,
In sylvan twilight's warm embrace,
The magic grants what hearts may choose.

So let your spirit dance and sway,
In dreams illuminated clear,
For in the night, we find our way,
Through forests deep, our paths endear.

Illumination in the Woodland Dusk

The twilight whispers through the trees,
Soft shadows dance with the evening breeze.
Fireflies twinkle like stars on the ground,
Magic in the air, a treasure unbound.

Moss carpets secrets that silence keeps,
While the heart of the forest gently weeps.
Moonbeams thread through branches above,
This dusk-lit realm, a cradle of love.

A chorus of crickets begins their song,
As night unfolds, where dreams belong.
Flickers of light guide the wandering feet,
In this serene place, where all souls meet.

Ancient oaks hold tales yet untold,
In the cool dusk air, their wisdom unfolds.
Creatures hidden, watching from afar,
Among the shadows, they too, are a star.

In the heart of dusk, enchantments are spun,
A tapestry woven before the day's done.
Hold your breath, for the night will embrace,
The woodland magic, in this sacred place.

Glinting Essence of the Elven Meadow

Beneath the sky where the sunlight bends,
A meadow blooms where time transcends.
Petals shimmer like gems in the light,
Whispering secrets of morning's delight.

Elven laughter dances on the breeze,
As flowers sway like gentle seas.
With glinting essence, their colors burst,
In this cherished glade, where hopes are nursed.

Dewdrops linger on blades of green,
Reflecting dreams that once were seen.
Here, magic weaves through every stem,
Nature's canvas, a vibrant gem.

As twilight descends, a spell shall rise,
Stars emerge in the velvet skies.
Though shadows grow, the heart stays bright,
In the elven meadow, love turns to light.

With each soft sigh of the whispering grass,
Time weaves tales that forever last.
In this glimmering realm, where spirits play,
The essence of magic guides the way.

Radiant Moondust on Leafy Canopy

In the heart of night, the forest sighs,
Where moonbeams glow and mysteries rise.
Radiant moondust spills from above,
Kissing the leaves with a tender love.

Whispers of night wrap the trees tight,
A shroud of magic embraces the night.
As darkness dances, shadows take flight,
Leading the way to the dawn's first light.

Branches sway soft, to a silent tune,
Beneath the gaze of the watchful moon.
Every rustle, a secret profound,
In this enchanted world, beauty is found.

The canopy shimmers with jeweled delight,
Every leaf cloaked in silvery light.
As dreams drift softly through hollows and nooks,
The heart finds its joy in the stillness of books.

In the stillness found beneath the vast sky,
The secrets of night invite a soft sigh.
In moondust's embrace, we find our place,
Wrapped in the magic, a tender grace.

Starlit Reveries in the Enchanted Realm

As twilight falls, the stars awake,
In the enchanted realm, where dreams partake.
Sparkling whispers spin through the air,
Casting a spell, woven with care.

Every twinkle tells a tale untold,
Of valiant hearts and adventures bold.
In the hush of night, possibilities soar,
In this starlit haven, we forever explore.

Velvet skies cradle the glimmering light,
Guiding lost souls through the cloak of night.
In shadows deep, where futures are spun,
A dance of fate, where we all become one.

Moonlit paths beckon, so soft, so bright,
Leading us onward in shimmering flight.
Each starlit reverie penned in the air,
A tapestry woven with wonder and care.

Awake in the magic, our spirits take wing,
To places untouched where the heart learns to sing.
In the enchanted realm, we find our dreams,
With starlit whispers and moonbeam gleams.

Fae Light in the Twilight Grove

In shadows deep, where whispers dwell,
A fae light weaves its magic spell.
Among the trees, in twilight's grace,
The night unfolds, a secret place.

With laughter soft, the leaves will sway,
As starlit dreams invite the play.
The glowing spheres like fireflies,
Guide wanderers with teasing sighs.

The brook sings low, a gentle tune,
Beneath the gaze of a silver moon.
The fae dance round, with joy in sight,
Their radiance a wondrous light.

Underneath the ancient oak,
Their hidden forms, in laughter spoke.
A moment sweet, time holds its breath,
In nature's arms, they charm from death.

As night gives way to morning's hue,
The fae retreat, yet leave a clue.
A path of glimmer, soft and bright,
A trace of magic in the light.

Dance of the Glowing Sylphs

In midnight's hush, the sylphs appear,
With twinkling eyes, they bring us near.
Their laughter floats on gentle breeze,
A symphony that puts hearts at ease.

With flowing gowns of twilight shade,
They swirl and glide, a grand parade.
Around the glen, they spin and twirl,
In nature's dance, the wonders unfurl.

Each flicker bright, a tale untold,
Of ancient woods and secrets bold.
Among the stars their spirits soar,
In every step, a whispered lore.

Illumined paths by fireflies' light,
Guide us to their enchanting sight.
With petals soft beneath our feet,
We join their dance, a blissful feat.

As dawn approaches, shadows wane,
The sylphs retreat but leave a stain.
A memory of magic's play,
To linger sweet until next day.

Beyond the Veil of Silver Glade

Where silver glades and whispers meet,
A world awakes, so pure and sweet.
Beyond the veil, in moonlit streams,
The heart will find its lostest dreams.

Soft echoes call with dulcet tones,
And secrets shared by ancient stones.
The hidden paths of twilight bloom,
In that stillness, dispels all gloom.

The silver mist dances and sways,
As twilight weaves its wondrous ways.
Each glowing orb, a guiding light,
To lead the lost through endless night.

With breathless awe, we take our place,
In nature's arms, in sweet embrace.
Beyond the veil, our souls take flight,
In harmony with the stars' delight.

As day breaks through the silent shroud,
The glade awakes, adorned and proud.
Yet in our hearts, the magic stays,
A treasure etched in twilight's gaze.

Flickering Echoes in the Moonlit Wild

In the wild, where shadows leap,
Flickering echoes gently creep.
By moon's warm glow, they stir the night,
Awakening dreams with their soft light.

In the thickets, whispers roam,
As creatures stir, they find their home.
The owls take flight, the stars align,
With every flicker, the heart will pine.

The silver brook reflects the sky,
As secrets weave and gently sigh.
Beneath the boughs, a tale unfolds,
Of ancient spirits and tales retold.

Across the glen, the echoes call,
A haunting song that fills it all.
With every note, the magic grows,
In moonlit wild, the wonder flows.

As night gives in to morning's kiss,
We hold the dream, an endless bliss.
For in the wild, where heartbeats blend,
The echoes linger, never end.

Luminescent Whispers Among the Trees

In the hush of twilight's grace,
The leaves softly whisper their lore,
A dance of shadows, a sacred space,
Where secrets of the forest soar.

Moonlight spills through branches wide,
Casting spells where dreams ignite,
Each rustling leaf a gentle guide,
Leading hearts to the starlit night.

Amidst the roots, the magic stirs,
With twinkling eyes of hidden sprites,
Each breeze a song, a world that purrs,
In whispers of the endless nights.

They weave a tapestry of green,
Where colors blend in softest hues,
Each flicker tells a tale unseen,
Of time-torn paths and ancient views.

So linger here, let the night unfurl,
Embrace the wonders nature brews,
In luminescent whispers, the world
Awakens dreams that time renews.

Celestial Fireflies in the Dreamscape

In the realm where slumbers weave,
The fireflies dance, a glowing spark,
Each flicker glints like hopes conceived,
In the quiet shadows, they embark.

Through fields of wonder, they take flight,
Painting wishes on the velvet sky,
Their luminescent grace ignites,
As dreams descend and softly sigh.

In this enchanted dreamscape fair,
They whisper tales of yesteryears,
Of gentle hearts that wander there,
And laughter mingled with our tears.

Beneath a canopy of starlit streams,
The fireflies twirl in joyful arcs,
Illuminating hidden dreams,
Their presence leaving glowing marks.

So let your heart take fleeting flight,
With every pulse of shimmering glow,
In celestial realms, embrace the night,
And weave your dreams in gentle flow.

Secrets Drifting in the Gossamer Air

Beneath the arch of sapphire skies,
The whispers weave through twilight's seam,
Secrets float on the evening sighs,
Drifting lightly like a silver dream.

Gossamer threads of light entwine,
In the soft embrace of breezes' dance,
They carry tales, both yours and mine,
In the fleeting shadow of a glance.

Each heartbeat echoes, tender yet clear,
As night unveils its velvet art,
Shimmering moments capturing dear,
The tender secrets of the heart.

Through rabbit holes of time and space,
The air is laden with stories old,
A gentle nudge, a fleeting trace,
Of wonders held, of truths untold.

So breathe the night, let secrets sing,
In gossamer whispers, find your way,
Each shimmering thread a wondrous thing,
A map of dreams we dare to sway.

Enchanted Glimmers Beneath the Stars

In the hush of night, the cosmos glows,
With glimmers that dance in ancient flight,
Each twinkle telling the tale it knows,
Of brave horizons and boundless light.

Beneath this vast, enchanted dome,
We wander lost in wonder's embrace,
Each star a beacon, a call to home,
In the stillness, we find our place.

The moon illuminates the whispered truth,
As shadows play in the fragrant air,
Echoes of joy and echoes of youth,
In enchanted glimmers, you are there.

With every pulse of starlit glow,
The universe breathes a timeless sigh,
A gentle nudge to let dreams flow,
And weave our fables across the sky.

So let your spirit soar and glide,
In the embrace of luminous night,
For in this realm, our hearts collide,
And write our stories in starlight bright.

Whispers of Luminous Dreams

In twilight's embrace, secrets unwind,
Voices of starlight, softly aligned.
They dance like shadows, in moon's gentle glow,
Guiding the lost, where few dare to go.

With each whispered tale, the night holds its breath,
A tapestry woven, from life unto death.
In dreams they flutter, like whispers of fate,
Carving their paths, both love and hate.

The flicker of candles, a sign from above,
Echoing memories, the warmth of lost love.
Through realms of enchantment, the heart learns to soar,
While wishes take flight, to open new doors.

So linger awhile, in this mystical space,
Where all are connected, in time's soft embrace.
Embrace the unknown, the curious gleams,
For life is but fabric, spun from our dreams.

In whispers we find, the strength to believe,
That magic is woven, in all that we grieve.
For light shall enact, its glorious scheme,
Illuminating paths, through luminous dreams.

Glimmers Through Enchanted Veils

Beneath the soft boughs of the willow tree,
Glimmers awaken, inviting the free.
Veils of enchantment, hung lightly in air,
Offer sweet secrets, to those who dare.

With steps like a whisper, the world starts to gleam,
Soft radiance spills, like a beautiful dream.
Unfolding the stories that twilight has spun,
Through flickers of hope, we embrace the sun.

Each sparkle a promise, each shimmer a call,
A touch of the magic that flows through us all.
Through enchanted veils, our spirits entwine,
In a dance of the cosmos, eternally divine.

The air sings with laughter, as shadows confess,
That joy is the path which we all must progress.
In moments of wonder, life's fabric we weave,
With glimmers of hope, we learn how to believe.

So wander with me, in this luminous night,
Where glimmers of beauty guide lost hearts to light.
Together we'll find, what we long to reveal,
In the magic that lies, through enchanted veils.

Ethereal Radiance in the Mist

Amidst the soft fog, where silence intrudes,
Ethereal light bathes the darkened woods.
Mysteries linger, like whispers unheard,
In the hush of the night, where nature's preferred.

With shadows in motion, the dancers appear,
Their movements like water, both fluid and clear.
Each breath of the mist, a tale yet untold,
In the heart of the forest, through ages of gold.

The glow of a lantern, a path through the gray,
Leading us gently, as night turns to day.
Among the tall trees, we wander and weave,
Embracing the magic, in which we believe.

Each moment a treasure, each heartbeat a gift,
In ethereal radiance, our spirits do lift.
As the dawn gently breaks, with its warm, tender kiss,
We awaken in wonder, wrapped in the mist.

So if you should find yourself lost in the night,
Trust in the glimmers, their soft, guiding light.
For magic surrounds us, in every twist,
In the depths of our hearts, ethereal mist.

Shimmering Threads of Nature's Magic

With each gentle breeze, we feel nature's breath,
Shimmering threads weave life into death.
The flowers bow low, their colors ablaze,
In the dance of the earth, we find truth in the maze.

From valleys to peaks, where the wild rivers glow,
In the forest's embrace, we witness the flow.
Nature's soft whispers, a chorus of grace,
Invite weary travelers to join in the race.

Each sunset a painting, brushed by the divine,
With hues of connection, and love intertwined.
The stars in their splendor, above us they gleam,
A reminder of magic, in each waking dream.

So gather the moments, let laughter unfold,
Through shimmering threads, our stories are told.
With open hearts, we'll embrace every sound,
In nature's own magic, true beauty is found.

As seasons keep turning, their cycles in play,
The threads remain strong, leading us on our way.
In moments of wonder, where love dares to play,
We find shimmering threads in nature's ballet.

The Flicker of Gossamer Wings

In twilight's breath, a dance begins,
With whispers soft like silken spins.
The fairies twirl in gentle flight,
Their laughter weaves through coming night.

Glimmers bright in dusky air,
A canvas painted of dreams laid bare.
Each brush of wing, a secret told,
In hues of silver, blue, and gold.

They flit and flutter, a lively sight,
In shadows deep, then taking flight.
They chase the stars, the moonlit streams,
Crafting stories from midnight dreams.

With every flicker, magic blooms,
In hidden corners and ancient rooms.
They weave enchantments, fate entwined,
In tender moments, love defined.

From dusk till dawn, they sing their song,
In the heart of woods where dreams belong.
The flicker fades as night turns day,
Yet in our hearts, they'll ever stay.

Glows Among the Elder Trees

Beneath the boughs of ancient lore,
Where wisdom sleeps on forest floor,
The whispers of the past resound,
In secret glades where dreams are found.

The elder trees, with knotted hands,
Guard tales of old in earthly strands.
Their leaves a canopy of light,
A sanctuary from the night.

Soft glows emerge from roots so deep,
Where shadows play and creatures creep.
The magic stirs in every breeze,
That dances through the elder trees.

In moonlit hours, they gather round,
The sprites and elves, in circles bound.
With laughter bright, they share their cheer,
A timeless bond that draws us near.

The night unfolds, a tale to spin,
Of heart and hope, where love begins.
In every glow, a wish takes flight,
Among the elder trees tonight.

Shards of Illumination Beneath the Canopy

In depths of wood, where shadows play,
The light breaks forth in bright array.
With shards of gold, the sun will shine,
A tapestry, both bold and fine.

Glimmers dance on leaves above,
Illuminating tales of love.
Each sparkle whispers secrets grand,
Lost moments cradled in time's hand.

Beneath the canopy, spirits glide,
With nature's grace as their guide.
They weave a world of endless light,
Where day and dreams entwine at night.

From roots to blooms, the magic flows,
In every leaf, the mystery grows.
Beyond the dark, in hues of bright,
The shards of joy, a pure delight.

As sunlight dims and stars ignite,
The forest breathes, a wondrous sight.
In every heart, a promise beams,
Of magic found in wispy dreams.

Radiant Revelry in the Fae Realm

In glades where time forgets its way,
The fae will come to dance and play.
With wings like petals, bright and bold,
They weave a tale of joy untold.

Their laughter rings like crystal chimes,
Resounding through the ancient rhymes.
In circles spun of starlit fate,
They gather close, they celebrate.

With moonbeams caught in silken threads,
They share their dreams as daylight spreads.
In every twirl, a secret sleeps,
Of magic's power, love that creeps.

Through emerald fields and sparkling streams,
They dance beneath the sun's soft beams.
In radiant hues of brilliant light,
The fae realm glimmers through the night.

As dusk drapes down its velvet cloak,
The laughter continues, never broke.
For in this realm of pure delight,
The fae's revelry ignites the night.

Mystical Luminance in Wisteria Aisles

In twilight's glow, the wisteria sway,
Petals shimmer, a soft purple array.
Whispers of magic dance in the breeze,
Promises kept beneath ancient trees.

Through tangled vines, secrets unfold,
A story of wonder, forever retold.
Glimmers of starlight, enchanting and bright,
Call forth the spirits of long-lost night.

Each step taken, a journey anew,
With laughter of fairies we venture through.
Misty enchantments, so sweetly they cling,
Awakening dreams that the dusk will bring.

In the heart of the grove where shadows play,
Lies a world where the mundane cannot stay.
With every heartbeat, the magic does rise,
In the mystical glow of the wisteria skies.

Dazzling Dreams in the Fairy's Abode

In a glen where the blossoms gleam,
Fairy laughter flows like a dream.
Sparkling dust in the soft moonlight,
Guides us gently into the night.

Beneath the boughs where the starlings sing,
Born of the dawn, our hopes take wing.
Petals of velvet, a tapestry spun,
Woven with warmth from the rise of the sun.

In this haven, where time stands still,
Magic awakens, our spirits to fill.
With glimmering eyes, the fairies parade,
We dance through the night, unafraid and uncrayed.

As dreams take form in the silver mist,
In every heartbeat, a sweet fairytale twist.
A world of wonder, forever we'll mold,
In the fairy's abode, where dreams are gold.

Sparks of Joy in the Twilight Glade

In the embrace of the twilight shade,
Where shadows whisper and glimmers fade.
Sparks of joy in the gentle air,
Glimpse of magic beyond compare.

Soft laughter echoes off trees so tall,
As glowing fireflies begin their thrall.
Each flicker a secret, aglow in the night,
Calling the stars to join in their flight.

The gossamer threads of dreams entwine,
Weaving bright tales in the soft moonshine.
Each moment a treasure, a memory made,
In the heart of the glade where joys never fade.

As evening falls, and the world takes rest,
Our hearts beat wildly, forever blessed.
In the twilight's embrace, we find our spark,
In a dance of wonder, we light the dark.

Celestial Whispers Beneath the Canopy's Veil

Amidst the leaves, where the starlight plays,
Celestial whispers weave through the haze.
In the cool of the night, knowledge bestowed,
Secrets of ages in dreams easily flowed.

Moonbeams dance on the forest floor,
Echoing stories of those gone before.
Under the canopy, in silence we sit,
Gathering echoes, each moment we knit.

The rustling leaves join the soft refrain,
As hearts beat together, like soothing rain.
With every sigh, a new tale ignites,
Beneath this vast web of endless nights.

In the arms of the night, with spirits entwined,
We travel through realms both gentle and blind.
Celestial whispers, a soft, secret song,
In nature's embrace, we forever belong.

Radiant Echoes of the Fey Realm

In whispers soft, the echoes dance,
Beneath a sky of emerald chance.
The glimmering paths where fairies tread,
Illuminate dreams where magic's bred.

With laughter light, they weave the night,
A tapestry spun with wonder and light.
Through twilight's veil, their secrets unfold,
In shimmering tales of the brave and bold.

The ancient woods, a guarded keep,
Holds stories deep where shadows creep.
Each rustling leaf, a gentle sigh,
Inviting souls to wander and fly.

With every step, a journey starts,
As moonbeams kiss the fey hearts.
Golden flames that flicker, spark,
In the realm where dreams leave a mark.

So seek the trails less traveled by,
In twilight's breath, let spirits soar high.
For in the fey, where wonders blend,
Radiance lingers, on it depend.

Gossamer Dreams Above the Sylvan Canopy

On velvet wings, the dreams take flight,
Above the woods, in the hush of night.
Gossamer threads of silver spun,
Glint and shimmer in the warmth of sun.

The branches sway with a timeless grace,
Welcoming whispers in this sacred space.
Each note and song, a secret shared,
A bond unbroken, where hearts laid bare.

Beneath a shroud of leafy lace,
The forest breathes in a slow embrace.
Magic lingers like the dew,
In every glade where the wildflowers grew.

A tapestry woven in hues so bright,
Illuminates dreams, igniting the night.
With gentle hands that reach and weave,
The sylvan canopy bids all to believe.

In the hush of dusk, where fairy lights gleam,
The world unfurls like a vivid dream.
Gossamer threads, like starlit sighs,
Guide us gently under azure skies.

Shimmering Essence in Moonlit Glades

In moonlit glades where shadows play,
The shimmering essence guides the way.
With silver beams that weave and flow,
An ethereal light in the twilight glow.

Here the secrets of the night unfold,
In whispers soft of dreams retold.
Elusive forms drift through the air,
Chasing glimmers, bright and rare.

The fragrant blooms release their charms,
Calling forth magic with open arms.
Glades alive with enchanting sights,
Paint the dark with radiant lights.

As fireflies twinkle in golden flight,
Hearts ignite with pure delight.
For in this realm where shadows cease,
The shimmering essence brings forth peace.

So tread with care where the moonbeams kiss,
In glades of wonder, find your bliss.
With every heartbeat, let magic reside,
In the shimmering essence of nature's guide.

Phantoms of Light in the Faerie Night

Where stars entwine with the velvet night,
Dance phantoms of light, wonderful and bright.
Their laughter echoes through shadows deep,
In a twilight realm where secrets keep.

With every flicker, dreams take shape,
In this enchanted world, there's no escape.
Twisting paths of luminescent glow,
Guide wandering souls with stories to sow.

The nightingale sings an ancient tune,
Under the watch of the watchful moon.
Each note a spell woven with care,
Filling the night with magic rare.

The faerie lights twinkle in unison bright,
Drawing all hearts to their dazzling sight.
In this place where wonders unfold,
Phantoms of light weave tales of old.

So linger here, let your spirit take flight,
With phantoms of light in the faerie night.
Embrace the spellbound, join in the dance,
For in this magic lies your chance.

Reflections of Light on the Forest Floor

In a hush, the soft sun beams,
Dance like fairies through the seams.
Leaves twinkle with whispers bright,
Caressing roots in golden light.

Mossy greens and browns entwined,
Nature's brush, a path defined.
Beneath the boughs, a world anew,
Where time drifts slow, and dreams come true.

Echoes of the forest's song,
In hidden nooks where heartbeats throng.
The air is thick with stories told,
Of magic realms and treasures bold.

As shadows stretch and twilight creeps,
The forest sighs, as daylight sleeps.
A silver glow begins to spread,
Awakening stars overhead.

Upon the floor, reflections play,
In murmurs soft, they weave and sway.
A tapestry of fleeting light,
Illuminating the forest night.

Flickers of Fantasy in the Whispering Night

Underneath a velvet sky,
Where stardust dreams and wishes fly.
Whispers weave through branches bare,
Magic lingers in the air.

Lanterns of the fireflies dance,
Casting shadows, a fleeting glance.
In twilight's hush, the world transforms,
And fantasy in silence swarms.

Mysterious glades, where secrets lay,
A cascade of echoes leads the way.
Every rustle, each sighing breeze,
Speaks of wonders, puts hearts at ease.

The moon, a guardian, ever bright,
Gilds the night with silver light.
Time pauses in this sacred space,
Holding dreams in a warm embrace.

Flickers of fate with secrets spun,
In the whispering night, we are one.
The heart of magic gently calls,
As fantasy in the darkness sprawls.

The Glow that Awakens the Enchanted

In glen so deep, where shadows meet,
An ember's glow ignites the sweet.
Firelight dances on ancient stone,
Awakens spirits, long unknown.

Beneath the stars, the forest sings,
Of whispered hopes and wondrous things.
With every flicker, life unfolds,
As magic whispers tales of old.

The trees sway softly, their leaves anew,
Breathing life into dreams that grew.
Each gentle flicker, a promise kept,
In this enchanted night, we've leapt.

As night embraces, the world ignites,
The glow connects our soaring flights.
With every heartbeat, every sigh,
The enchanted weave, the times gone by.

Awaken now, dear wandering soul,
Let the light envelop your whole.
In this dusk, a magic's spun,
In the glow, we find our one.

Elysian Flickers Among the Shadows

Elysian lights in night's embrace,
Hide from time, in gentle grace.
Among the shadows, soft they play,
Whispers of night that drift away.

Each flicker hints at stories grand,
Of realms where dreams and wishes stand.
A tapestry of flick'ring glows,
Guides the wishful heart that knows.

With every breath, the silence hums,
In echoes sweet, the magic drums.
A brush of light, a touch divine,
Where age-old shadows intertwine.

The moonlight weaves a silver thread,
Through realms where even lost dreams tread.
In this embrace, with tender care,
Elysian wonders weave the air.

Among the shadows, we shall find,
The flickers of the heart and mind.
In this enchanted midnight glow,
The dance of dreams will always flow.

Glimmering Realities of the Sylvan Light

In woods where shadows softly meld,
Glimmers of magic gently held.
With whispers from the trees nearby,
The secrets of the forest sigh.

Each leaf doth shimmer, each branch does gleam,
A world alive, a vivid dream.
Beneath the boughs, where spirits dwell,
The stories of the wilds we tell.

Moments frozen, time stands still,
In realms where wonder bends our will.
The paths unworn, the colors bright,
Glimmering truths in sylvan light.

Upon the breeze, sweet scents arise,
As sunlight dances in the skies.
The heart of nature sings so clear,
A melody for all to hear.

So tread with awe, oh, wanderer bold,
In glimmering woods, let tales unfold.
For magic weaves through every night,
In the embracing arms of gentle light.

Celestial Dances of Fairy Glimmers

Underneath the starry dome,
Fairies twirl, their hearts a-home.
With every spark, they paint the air,
Creating wonders beyond compare.

In midnight's hush, they twinkle bright,
Lost in the joy of pure delight.
They laugh and sing, their voices low,
As shimmering winds begin to blow.

Each flicker holds a dream, a wish,
A moment's treasure, a secret swish.
Through the veils of night, they soar,
With glistening paths to explore.

Through fields of twilight, soft and sweet,
They dance where earth and heaven meet.
With every flicker, shadows glide,
As stars come forth to be their guide.

So pause, dear friend, and watch the scene,
Where magic weaves through every green.
In the celestial dance of night,
Find solace in their twinkling light.

Aetherial Glow in the Heart of Night

Beneath the moon's soft silver gaze,
The night unfolds in mystic ways.
Aetherial glow surrounds the trees,
As shadows whisper with the breeze.

In stillness spreads the velvet dark,
Where fireflies ignite a spark.
Each flicker tells of timeless lore,
Inviting dreams forevermore.

The heart of night, a canvas broad,
Sings of secrets that we laud.
With gentle tides of whispered night,
We wander through its tranquil light.

Upon the edge of every thought,
Lies magic only dreamers sought.
With stars as jewels in a crown,
The universe holds us gently down.

So close your eyes and breathe it in,
Feel the warmth beneath the skin.
In aetherial glow, we find our might,
Embraced in the heart of night.

Shining Sentinels of the Fae

In glades where morning dew does kiss,
Stand guardians of a hidden bliss.
The sentinels of faerie lore,
Watch over all, forevermore.

With wings adorned in nature's hues,
They weave the threads of ancient views.
In silence, they protect the flow,
Of whispered dreams that softly grow.

By shimmering streams they take their stand,
A gentle force, a guiding hand.
With every flutter, harmony sings,
As magic blooms on delicate wings.

They dance upon the sunlit glade,
In shadows cast, their forms will fade.
Yet in their eyes, the stories lie,
Of all the worlds that touch the sky.

So heed their call, oh, wanderers brave,
The shining sentinels, they pave.
With hearts aglow, they light the way,
In realms where faeries laugh and play.

Captured Glimpses of Wonder's Heart

In twilight's hush, when dreams take flight,
The whispers dance, a soft delight.
A tapestry of time unwinds,
And magic's linger in our minds.

Through tangled woods where shadows play,
A glimmer leads the lost astray.
With every step, the heart will soar,
To places veiled, forevermore.

In laughter's wake, the moments gleam,
As starlit stories weave a dream.
Each glance, a spark, ignites the night,
A tapestry of purest light.

The echoes of a distant song,
In golden hues where we belong.
With every breath, the wonder grows,
Each captured glimpse, the heart bestows.

Through portals wide, where wonders blend,
The tales of old, we now defend.
In every soul, a tale does spark,
A captured glimpse, a beating heart.

Sparkling Serenity in the Heart of Dusk

When daylight dims and shadows fall,
The world transforms, a soft enthrall.
A hush descends, the stars awake,
In twilight's grace, our hearts partake.

The velvet skies, a canvas vast,
Where fleeting moments weave the past.
A whisper floats on gentle air,
As peace enfolds the evening rare.

The stillness holds a secret sigh,
As dreams unfurl and time slips by.
In every breath, serenity,
In dusk's embrace, our spirits free.

Each flicker glows, a guiding light,
In darkest hours, it sparkles bright.
A silent wish, the night unfurls,
As hope ignites and softly swirls.

With every heartbeat, magic sways,
In tranquil tunes, the soul obeys.
Sparkling serenity, a blissful dance,
In twilight's arms, we take our chance.

Lightborn Tales Among the Faerie Realms

In hidden glades where whispers tread,
The lightborn tales of faeries spread.
With silver wings, they flit and glide,
In every heart, their dreams abide.

Upon the breeze, their laughter flows,
A symphony where magic glows.
With twinkling eyes and hearts so bold,
They weave the stories yet untold.

Through meadows fair, the flowers sway,
As faerie folk dance night and day.
Each tale a spark, a thread of fate,
In realms where love and wonder wait.

The moonlit paths, where shadows weave,
Embrace the dreams that we believe.
A glimmer here, a shimmer there,
In every step, the magic's spare.

Among the stars, their voices sing,
Of joy and hope that love will bring.
Lightborn tales, forever shared,
In faerie realms, our hearts laid bare.

Ethereal Brilliance of Nature's Breath

In morning's light, where whispers bloom,
Ethereal thoughts break darkness' gloom.
The world awakens, vibrant, new,
Nature's pulse, a sacred view.

Through rustling leaves, the story flows,
Of ancient lands where beauty grows.
The rivers hum a timeless tune,
As sunlight dances, kissed by noon.

Each petal shines with colors bright,
A canvas brushed with pure delight.
In mountain heights, the echoes swell,
A symphony that weaves the spell.

Beneath the stars, the night ignites,
With constellations' whispered lights.
Ethereal dreams glide through the dark,
As nature's breath ignites the spark.

With every heartbeat, echoes weave,
The stories of the hearts that cleave.
Ethereal brilliance, pure and wide,
In nature's arms, we shall abide.

Celestial Flares in the Garden of Enchantment

In twilight's breath, the stars ignite,
Whispers bloom in silver light.
Petals dance with dreams untold,
In a garden where magic unfolds.

Crickets serenade the moon's embrace,
Each shadow shifts with gentle grace.
Luminous orbs like fireflies sing,
Gifting the night a tender fling.

The air is thick with fragrant spells,
A scribe of secrets that nature tells.
Among the thorns, a glimmer glows,
Guiding lost hearts where wonder flows.

Beneath the boughs, a tapestry spins,
Of laughter, love, where the heart begins.
Celestial flares chart a course,
In every leaf, the universe source.

Adventure blooms in each secret nook,
As starlight whispers in a storybook.
In this garden, enchantment thrives,
Where time dissolves, and magic survives.

Bioluminescent Tales from the Woodland's Edge

In silken night, the woods awake,
With glowing trails, the shadows break.
Whispers echo through twisting trees,
Bioluminescent tales ride the breeze.

Beneath warm boughs, the fungi gleam,
Casting light like a moonlit dream.
Creatures flutter, tales unsung,
In every glimmer, a story young.

Mossy carpets hold secrets tight,
Where fireflies dance in sporadic flight.
The owl hoots softly, a guardian wise,
Beneath the glow of starry skies.

In this land where shadows pulse,
Whimsical hopes and fears convulse.
Every glow whispers of fate,
Crafting yarns that softly narrate.

From edges dark, where wonders meet,
Each flicker leads on nimble feet.
Tales born of night, forever bright,
In the heart of woods, spreading light.

Flashes of Laughter in Faerie Realms

Through gossamer threads of twilight haze,
Laughter bubbles in the faerie's phase.
Glimmering wings in joyful flight,
In realms where magic dances light.

Giggling sprites chase shadows bold,
With secrets spun from marigold.
Moonbeams weave a soft refrain,
In an echo of joy, they remain.

Sprinkled stardust on every grin,
Where mischief lies and dreams begin.
Fairy rings in dew-tipped grass,
Holding the moments as hours pass.

Wandering souls in whispering trees,
Join in the song upon the breeze.
In faerie realms, each laugh's a start,
A tapestry woven from the heart.

With every twinkle, laughter's cry,
Entwines the night, paints the sky.
In such splendor, we all can seem,
To glimpse the magic of every dream.

Aurora's Touch on Ethereal Blossoms

In dawn's embrace, the colors flare,
Aurora's touch on blossoms rare.
A gentle blush in morning's sigh,
As petals wake to greet the sky.

Shades of amber, pink, and gold,
Whisper secrets, tales unfold.
In gardens born of magic's charm,
Nature weaves its soft alarm.

Rippling dew like diamonds lies,
Catching visions in waking eyes.
Every bloom a silent plea,
For wonders hidden, wild and free.

As sunlight spills through leafy lanes,
Auroras dance in soft refrains.
Each bloom, a story yet to weave,
In the heart of daylight, we believe.

So let us linger, feel the grace,
In every flower, a sacred space.
For with each dawn, the world anew,
Awaits our dreams to break through.

Whispers of Celestial Glimmers

In stillness wrapped, the stars do gleam,
Whispers soft, like a waking dream.
A dance of light on the silken night,
Each twinkle tells of ancient flight.

A tapestry spun with threads of gold,
Secrets of cosmos, silently told.
Veils of shimmer in twilight drift,
Soft voices of shadow, a silvery gift.

Each breath of wind carries a plea,
From depths of space, wild and free.
The heartbeats echo in blissful rhyme,
As night unfolds, welcoming time.

Glimmers fade, yet do not cease,
In every whisper, there lies peace.
Look to the heavens, with eyes aglow,
For through the dark, the light will flow.

So hush now, dear, and close your eyes,
Feel the magic across the skies.
For in the silence, dreams ignite,
In whispers bright, the stars take flight.

Glades of Elven Light

Beneath the boughs where shadows play,
Elven laughter lights the way.
A glade adorned in emerald hue,
With secrets wrapped in morning dew.

Soft petals dance on the gentle breeze,
Whispers echo through ancient trees.
A realm where time appears to pause,
Nature's magic, a silent cause.

Glistening streams with laughter run,
Cradle the light of the golden sun.
Elven eyes, like stars, do shine,
Binding hearts, both yours and mine.

Mossy stones tell tales of yore,
While hidden paths invite us more.
In every rustle, a song is found,
In Glades of Light, our dreams unbound.

So linger here, where wonders weave,
In every corner, magic breathes.
For in this place of pure delight,
We dance together in elven light.

Luminous Threads in Enchanted Woodland

Through branches thick, a soft glow spreads,
Threads of light where adventure treads.
Beneath the canopy, secrets lie,
Whispering softly, as night draws nigh.

Moss-carpeted paths, a tender sigh,
Where glowing orbs like fireflies fly.
Every flicker tells a story anew,
Of woodland dreams, both brave and true.

Gathered fog wraps the earth in mist,
In every breath, magic is kissed.
The trees stand tall, their wisdom vast,
Guardians of future, present, past.

With every rustle, the night does play,
Enchanted moments beckon to stay.
Luminous threads in the cool night air,
Weaving tales with silken care.

So wander through these woods so grand,
With heart wide open, take my hand.
For in this realm where wonders blend,
Our spirits soar, our joys transcend.

Ethereal Flickers in Twilight's Embrace

As day surrenders to night's soft hold,
Ethereal flickers, a sight to behold.
In twilight's arms, shadows entwine,
Gathering magic 'neath the silver line.

Every heartbeat, a gentle call,
Celestial whispers in the fall.
Stars awaken, a subtle ignite,
Guiding the lost through the velvet night.

A chorus of crickets, the night's sweet song,
Drawing the dreamers who wander along.
Mist hugs the earth with a tender kiss,
In twilight's embrace, we find our bliss.

So listen closely to the night's refrain,
In ethereal flickers, there's no more pain.
Revel in moments that softly sway,
For in this dusk, our spirits play.

With each fading light, new dreams ignite,
In the warmth of whispers, we find our light.
So hold me near, as shadows trace,
Together we dance in twilight's embrace.

Luminary Dreams on Glistening Petals

In twilight's embrace, dreams take flight,
Glistening petals catch the soft light.
Each whisper of magic dances around,
As moonbeams shimmer on the ground.

Nights filled with wonder, secrets untold,
In gardens of starlight, mysteries unfold.
A tapestry woven with hope and with grace,
In the heart of the night, we find our place.

Dreamers unite under skies so vast,
With wishes so bright, our shadows are cast.
A flicker, a flutter, in silence they gleam,
With luminary dreams wrapped in a dream.

Together we wander, through fields made of dreams,
Where magic ignites, and nothing's as it seems.
On paths of enchantment, with each gentle sigh,
We float like the whispers, where lost spirits fly.

So let us remember, with hearts open wide,
The glistening petals, our souls as our guide.
In realms forged by starlight, we'll always reside,
In luminary dreams, our spirits collide.

Shining Threads of Enchantment

Woven in twilight, the stars gently gleam,
Shining threads of enchantment, a delicate dream.
In shadows of wonder, we weave and we spin,
Crafting our fortunes, where magic begins.

Each flicker of light, a story unfolds,
Tales of the heart that rapture and hold.
With whispers like silk, soft secrets align,
Creating a tapestry, endlessly divine.

The dance of the fireflies, bright in the night,
Guiding lost wanderers with shimmering light.
In gardens of wonder, where wishes take flight,
We find our enchantment, in love's gentle sight.

So grasp, dear dreamers, these threads spun of gold,
In the fabric of night, we'll be ever bold.
In shimmering silence, our souls intertwine,
As shining threads of enchantment align.

With joyous hearts, let the magic ignite,
In the realm of the dreamers, forever in flight.
Together, we'll weave through the shadows and light,
Entwined in this dance, our spirits alight.

Melody of Glowing Essence

In forests enchanted, a melody flows,
Of glowing essence, where soft magic grows.
The breeze holds a tune, so sweet and so rare,
As notes drape the twilight, casting spells in the air.

Each whisper of night carries songs from the trees,
With harmonies echoing, carried by the breeze.
In flickers of moonlight, the melody sways,
Drawing the heart into ethereal plays.

With voices of shadows, serenades blend,
In the chambers of silence, where spirits transcend.
The dance of the fireflies mirrors the song,
A rhythm unbroken, inviting us along.

So close your eyes softly, let the music embrace,
Feel the heartbeat of nature, a timeless space.
For in this glow, we discover our essence,
A harmony whispered in quiet presence.

Embrace the sweet magic, let kindness arise,
In the melody of life, beneath endless skies.
With glowing essence, our spirits take wing,
In the symphony of wonders, together we sing.

Fae Whispers in the Stillness of Night

In the stillness of night, where dreams softly tread,
Fae whispers unravel, as starlight is spread.
Through the hush of the twilight, their laughter takes flight,
Guiding the lost with a spark of pure light.

In moonlit glades, where the shadows entwine,
The essence of magic begins to align.
With every soft rustle, a promise is made,
As fae set the rhythm for magical trade.

Emerald glimmers dance softly on air,
Each glittering moment, a breath of rare flare.
They weave tales of wonder, in flickers and stars,
With wisdom of ages woven into their bars.

So come, gentle dreamers, explore this delight,
In realms where the fae sing their songs through the night.

Let wonder be your guide, with each tender sigh,
For in fae whispers, our spirits will fly.

Forever we'll cherish these moments divine,
Together, we wander where magic aligns.
In the stillness of night, with hearts open wide,
We'll dance with the fae, as the stars collide.

The Glow Beneath the Silver Leaves

In twilight's hush, the whispers sing,
Of secrets held in leaf and wing.
A soft, ethereal light descends,
Where silver boughs and magic blends.

The forest breathes a gentle sigh,
While twinkling stars adorn the sky.
Each flicker tells of tales long past,
As shadows in the twilight cast.

Beneath the trees where dreams take flight,
The glow reveals the hidden sight.
A dance of faeries, wild and free,
A glimpse of what is yet to be.

With every step, the heart beats fast,
In this enchantment, love is cast.
The silver leaves a canopy,
Where wishes bloom in harmony.

So wander forth through dusk's embrace,
And let the magic set its pace.
For in this land of joy and grace,
The glow beneath shall leave its trace.

Echoes of Light in the Enchanted Vale

A vale where echoes softly play,
In twilight's weave, they dance and sway.
The woods alive with whispered tune,
Beneath the gaze of a silvery moon.

Each shadow weaves a story bright,
In whispers carried by the night.
The gentle breeze, a subtle guide,
As mystic paths in darkness bide.

The light enchants, a fleeting glance,
Inviting all to join the dance.
With every step, the spirits call,
In the vale's embrace, we'll never fall.

The glimmering orbs begin to rise,
As laughter bubbles, sweet surprise.
In every heart, the warmth ignites,
In echoes of light, pure delight.

So linger here, lose track of time,
In nature's song, a perfect rhyme.
The Enchanted Vale, forever stilled,
With echoes of light, our dreams fulfilled.

Illuminated Paths of the Sylvan Spirits

In emerald groves, the spirits dwell,
With stories wrapped in nature's spell.
The paths illuminated, soft and bright,
They guide the wanderers through the night.

Each glowing step, a promise made,
Through misty trails where dreams cascade.
With laughter ringing like crystal chimes,
The sylvan whispers fall in rhymes.

Beneath the arches woven tight,
The shimmering trails gleam in sight.
The woodland creatures pause and stare,
As magic dances in the air.

In every shadow, a spark of joy,
With fairy lights that never cloy.
These paths where fate and fortune blend,
To every heart, the spirits send.

So take this journey, sweet and free,
In twilight's arms, just you and me.
For in this realm of light and cheer,
The sylvan spirits draw us near.

Ethereal Glow on the Sylph's Trail

On sylph's trail where starlight weaves,
An ethereal glow entwines the leaves.
Each shimmer sparkles in the night,
A guiding light, a wondrous sight.

The air is laced with fragrant dreams,
And moonlit rays dance in soft beams.
With every footfall, magic blooms,
As nightingale within softly croons.

The sylphs are laughing, pure delight,
Their laughter echoing in flight.
Through fragrant fields, they twirl and glide,
A harmony where spirits bide.

With silver trails that twist and turn,
The heart, enchanted, starts to yearn.
For in this world of wonderland,
The sylph's embrace, a gentle hand.

So follow where the glow leads on,
Through moonlit dreams till velvet dawn.
In stillness find each hidden grace,
On sylph's trail, our souls embrace.